from SEA TO SHINING SEA

NEW HAMPSHIRE

By Dennis Brindell Fradin

CONSULTANTS

William Copeley, Librarian, New Hampshire Historical Society

Maryann Lacasse, Elementary Facilitator, Rochester, New Hampshire Schools; New Hampshire Studies Consultant

Robert L. Hillerich, Ph.D., Consultant, Pinellas County Schools, Florida; Visiting Professor, University of South Florida

CHILDREN'S PRESS
A Division of Grolier Publishing
New York London Hong Kong Sydney
Danbury, Connecticut

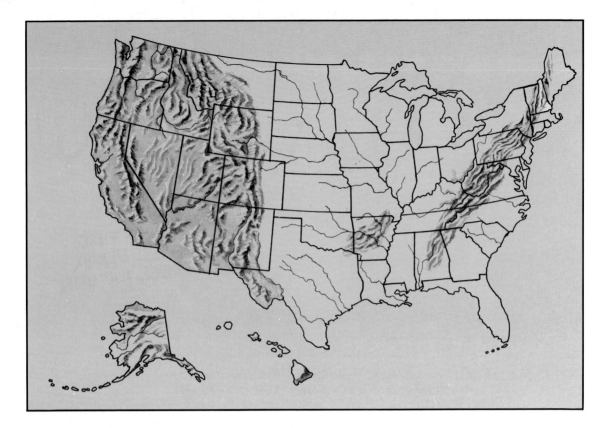

New Hampshire is one of the six states in the region called New England. The other New England states are Connecticut, Maine, Massachusetts, Rhode Island, and Vermont.

For my niece, Rebecca Fradin Polster—one of my favorite states for one of my favorite people

Front cover picture: Highland Lake, East Andover; page 1, Cornish-Windsor Covered Bridge; back cover, fall color in Andover

Project Editor: Joan Downing
Design Director: Karen Kohn
Research Assistant: Judith Bloom Fradin
Typesetting: Graphic Connections, Inc.
Engraving: Liberty Photoengraving

FOURTH PRINTING, 1995.

Copyright © 1992 Childrens Press®, Inc.
All rights reserved. Published simultaneously in Canada.
Printed in the United States of America.
    4 5 6 7 8 9 10 R 01 00 99 98 97 96 95

Library of Congress Cataloging-in-Publication Data

Fradin, Dennis B.
    New Hampshire / by Dennis Brindell Fradin.
        p.   cm. — (From sea to shining sea)
    Includes index.
    Summary: An overview of the Granite State, introducing its history, geography, industries, sites of interest, and famous people.
    ISBN 0-516-03829-X
    1. New Hampshire—Juvenile literature. [1. New Hampshire.] I. Title. II. Series: Fradin, Dennis B. From sea to shining sea.
F34.3.F69   1992   92-9216
974.2—dc20   CIP
                                                         AC

Table of Contents

A sled ride in the snow

INTRODUCING THE GRANITE STATE

New Hampshire is in the northeastern United States. It lies along the Atlantic Ocean. New Hampshire is tiny. Its population is also small. Yet, few places on earth can match its beauty. The state is filled with lovely woods, lakes, and mountains.

New Hampshire is called the "Granite State." The very hard rock called granite lies under most of its land. The state's settlers were as tough as granite, too. English people began arriving in 1623. They overcame many hardships to build New Hampshire.

In 1776, New Hampshire became the first colony to break from England. New Hampshirites then helped the United States win the Revolutionary War. One of them was General John Stark.

During the 1800s, New Hampshirites were leaders in the fight to end slavery. More recently, New Hampshire produced two famous space travelers: Alan B. Shepard, Jr., and Christa McAuliffe.

There is much more that is special about the Granite State. What state's vote put the United

States Constitution into effect? Where were President Franklin Pierce and statesman Daniel Webster born? Where did the author of "Mary Had a Little Lamb" live? What state had the strongest wind ever measured on earth? The answer to all of those questions is: New Hampshire!

A picture map of New Hampshire

Overleaf: A Bristol farmer with his oxen

DUNNINGTON

A Land of Mountains, Woods, and Lakes

A Land of Mountains, Woods, and Lakes

New Hampshire is a New England state. Besides New Hampshire, New England contains Massachusetts, Connecticut, Maine, Rhode Island, and Vermont. All six New England states are small. Only six states in the nation are smaller than New Hampshire.

New Hampshire looks like a slice of pie that wasn't cut straight. This is caused by the Connecticut River and Halls Stream. They form New Hampshire's western border. Vermont lies across this western border. So does Quebec, in Canada. Quebec also forms New Hampshire's northern border. Massachusetts is to the south. Maine and an 18-mile stretch of the Atlantic Ocean

Vermont looks like an upside-down New Hampshire.

Queen Anne's lace brightens the ocean shore at Rye.

TOPOGRAPHY

5,000 m. | 2,000 m. | 1,000 m. | 500 m. | 200 m. | 100 m. | Sea | Below
16,404 ft. | 6,562 ft. | 3,281 ft. | 1,640 ft. | 656 ft. | 328 ft. | Level

are to the east. The Isles of Shoals are a few miles offshore. The three southernmost of these rocky islands are part of New Hampshire. The other six islands are part of Maine.

Left: The "Boot Spur" at Pinkham Notch, Mount Washington

GEOGRAPHY

New Hampshire is rather flat for a few miles inland from the ocean. Most of the rest of the state is hilly or mountainous. The White Mountains cover most of New Hampshire's northern half. Mount Washington is in the White Mountains. It is the state's tallest peak. At 6,288 feet, it is the highest peak in all New England.

Some passes, or gaps, cut through New Hampshire's mountains. In New Hampshire, these gaps are called "notches." The Old Man of the Mountains stands in Franconia Notch. This famous rock formation looks like an old man's head.

Below: Fall colors, Wilmot

New Hampshire is known for its peaceful, blue lakes. The largest is Lake Winnipesaukee. It covers about 70 square miles. Some other lakes in the state are Sunapee, Ossipee, and the three Connecticut Lakes.

The Connecticut River is the state's longest river. It begins in far northern New Hampshire at the Connecticut Lakes. The river makes a 407-mile journey. Then it empties into Long Island Sound.

Left: Boats moored on Lake Winnipesaukee Right: Winneweta Falls, in Jackson

Above: The
Androscoggin River
Below: Pink lupines
and daisies in
Franconia Notch State
Park

This is part of the Atlantic Ocean south of the state of Connecticut. The Merrimack, Piscataqua, Androscoggin, Pemigewasset, and Saco are among the state's other rivers.

When seen from the air in the summer, New Hampshire is a sea of green. Eight-tenths of the state is made up of forests. Maine is the only state with a larger percentage of woodlands. Some trees that grow in New Hampshire are ashes, birches, pines, and spruces.

CLIMATE

Because New Hampshire is so far north, its climate is cool. Winter temperatures often dip below 0 degrees Fahrenheit. New Hampshire's record low was minus 46 degrees Fahrenheit. This occurred at Pittsburg, in the state's northern tip, on January 28, 1925. During the winter, New Hampshire usually wears a heavy coat of snow. Some mountain areas get 100 inches of snow yearly. Because of the heavy snows, skiers like to come to New Hampshire.

The state's record high temperature was 106 degrees Fahrenheit. Nashua set this record on the Fourth of July, 1911. However, most summer days are cool and comfortable. Typical summer temperatures are about 70 degrees Fahrenheit. Many people from hotter places visit New Hampshire in the summer to cool off.

Left: Winter on a farm in the White Mountains
Right: Spring in the woods near New London

From Ancient Times Until Today

FROM ANCIENT TIMES UNTIL TODAY

About two million years ago, the Ice Age began. Glaciers covered the northern part of North America. These slow-moving ice sheets covered all of New Hampshire. The glaciers deepened river valleys. Later, these valleys filled with water to become lakes. The glaciers also left a layer of granite rock on the land.

In places, the glaciers were more than a mile thick.

AMERICAN INDIANS

The Ice Age ended about 10,000 years ago. By that time, ancient Indians had reached New Hampshire. They moved about while hunting deer and bears. American Indian relics have been found at Lake Winnipesaukee. Some of them are more than 9,000 years old.

Much later, groups of Algonquian Indians lived in New Hampshire. They included the Ossipee, Nashua, Piscataqua, Pequacket, and Coosuc. Those American Indians also hunted and fished. But they also grew corn, beans, and squash. Farming allowed them to settle in villages.

Long ago, settlers pushed most of the American

Opposite: A July 1889 picture of farmers gathering hay at the Walker farm, Concord

15

Indians out of New Hampshire. Today, only about 2,000 American Indians live in the Granite State.

EXPLORERS

Historians aren't sure who first explored New Hampshire. The Vikings may have come first. They were people from Norway and nearby lands. The Vikings may have visited parts of New England around the year 1000.

Englishman Martin Pring was the first known explorer in New Hampshire. In 1603, he and his crew explored New England's coast from Maine to Massachusetts. French explorer Samuel de Champlain came in 1605.

In 1607, Captain John Smith arrived to settle the region. He helped found Jamestown, Virginia. It was England's first American town. Then, in 1614, Smith explored New England. He visited the

In 1614, Captain John Smith explored the New Hampshire coast (below).

New Hampshire coast and the Isles of Shoals. Smith wrote a book called *A Description of New England*. The book was read with great interest. It helped attract English people to the area.

ENGLAND'S THIRD AMERICAN COLONY

In 1622, Scotsman David Thomson received a grant of land in New Hampshire. He brought a small group of colonists to New Hampshire in 1623. They began a settlement at what is now the town of Rye. It was called Pannaway Plantation. It lasted only a few years.

Around this time, other English colonists began another settlement nearby. Edward and William Hilton were its founders. They were two brothers from London. The Hiltons' settlement became the town of Dover.

By 1623, New Hampshire was the third of England's thirteen colonies. Only Virginia and Massachusetts were settled earlier.

In 1622, a large amount of New England was granted to John Mason and Ferdinando Gorges. The two Englishmen divided this land in 1629. Gorges's land became part of Maine. Mason's became part of New Hampshire.

Captain John Smith

Dover still exists, but Pannaway Plantation lasted only a few years.

Strawbery Banke (above), now restored, is the colonial seaport that later became the city of Portsmouth.

In 1631, some English colonists sent by Mason began a town at a place where wild strawberries grew. They called their town Strawbery Banke. It was later named Portsmouth.

Most of New Hampshire's early settlers came because they wanted land. But some Massachusetts people came for religious freedom. In 1638, the Reverend John Wheelwright founded Exeter. That same year, Hampton was founded by other Massachusetts people. By 1640, New Hampshire had about 1,000 people. There were four coastal towns. They were Dover, Strawbery Banke, Exeter, and Hampton.

The four New Hampshire towns were too small to stand by themselves. For that reason, New Hampshire became part of the Massachusetts Bay

Colony in 1641. In 1673, a fifth New Hampshire town was founded. It was called Dunstable. The name was later changed to Nashua. Then, in 1679, the king of England made New Hampshire a separate colony.

The Growing Colony

New Hampshire grew—but slowly. By 1700, the colony had just 5,000 settlers. There were several reasons why more people didn't move there. New Hampshire's farmland had to be cleared of trees. It also had large rocks that the glaciers had left behind. Its winters were cold and snowy. Its soil wasn't very good for growing crops.

The hardy people who moved to New Hampshire cleared their fields of trees and rocks. They used the wood to build homes and furniture. They made low stone walls with the rocks. Those walls can still be seen throughout New Hampshire. The settlers fed themselves by hunting, fishing, and growing corn and beans. New Hampshirites also traded furs, fish, and lumber to England.

By the early 1700s, settlers were moving inland from the seacoast. Manchester (originally called Derryfield) was settled in 1722. Concord (originally

A typical New Hampshire stone wall

called Pennycook) was founded in 1727. It is now the capital. By 1732, New Hampshire had thirty-eight towns. There were about 12,000 settlers.

In 1719, people from Ireland founded Londonderry. They began growing potatoes. Soon, potatoes were a major crop in America. New Hampshire's first newspaper was founded at Portsmouth in 1756. It was called the *New Hampshire Gazette*. The colony's first stagecoach line began in 1761. New Hampshire's first college was founded at Hanover in 1769. It was named Dartmouth College.

In 1741, the king appointed Benning Wentworth royal governor. Wentworth granted hundreds of thousands of acres of land for settle-

New Hampshire's early farmers had to clear the rocks and stones from their land before they could plant crops.

ment. Wentworth resigned in 1766. By then, New Hampshire's population had grown to 52,000.

Up to that time, most New Hampshirites felt loyal to England. Hundreds of them had helped England win the French and Indian War (1754-1763). This war was fought between England and France. Both countries wanted to control the land and the fur trade in North America. Groups of American Indians sided with the French.

New Hampshire's Robert Rogers was a hero of the French and Indian War. He had a band of fighting men. They called themselves Rogers' Rangers.

THE REVOLUTIONARY WAR

The French and Indian War had cost the English a lot. Now they had to raise money. So England began taxing the American colonists.

The colonists hated those taxes. At first, they just protested. But then they became fighting mad. On December 14, 1774, four hundred New Hampshire patriots raided an English fort near Portsmouth. This was one of the Americans' first warlike acts against England.

On April 19, 1775, the Revolutionary War (1775-1783) began in Massachusetts. Americans fought it to break free of England. New Hampshire was the only colony where no battles were fought. But thousands of New Hampshirites fought elsewhere.

The Battle of Bunker Hill was fought in Boston on June 17, 1775. The Americans did much harm to the English in that battle. More than half of the 2,000 Americans there were from New Hampshire. They included Colonel John Stark.

Later, Stark was named a general. In 1777, he led New Englanders at the Battle of Bennington. That great American victory took place at the Vermont-New York border.

New Hampshire also built ships for the war. One of them was the *Ranger*. It was commanded by John Paul Jones. In 1777, the *Ranger* became the first warship to fly the American flag.

New Hampshire adopted its own constitution on January 5, 1776. It was no longer under English rule. New Hampshire was the first colony to do that. Then, on July 4, 1776, American leaders approved the Declaration of Independence. That paper said that the former thirteen colonies were now the United States of America. Josiah Bartlett, William Whipple, and Matthew Thornton signed it for New Hampshire.

Colonel John Stark

New Hampshire's troops fought in the battle that finally won the war. That was the Battle of Yorktown, in Virginia. George Washington's American army won the Battle of Yorktown in October 1781. The peace treaty that ended the war was signed in 1783.

BECOMING A STATE

At first, the United States government was weak. It was governed under the Articles of Confederation. In 1787, American leaders decided to create a stronger framework of government. They wrote the United States Constitution. John Langdon and Nicholas Gilman signed it for New Hampshire.

Each of the thirteen states was to approve or reject the Constitution. Approval meant the state was under the new government. The approval of nine states was needed.

By the spring of 1788, eight states had given their approval. On June 21, 1788, New Hampshire's leaders approved the Constitution. New Hampshire became the ninth state. The Constitution became the law of the land. In 1808, Concord became New Hampshire's permanent capital.

John Langdon was one of the New Hampshire signers of the Constitution. He later became governor of the state.

23

SLAVERY AND CIVIL WAR

There were never more than a few hundred slaves in New Hampshire.

During the early 1800s, Americans argued over slavery. All thirteen colonies had allowed slavery. But by the 1820s, it was outlawed in New Hampshire and the other northern states. The slavery question threatened to divide the northern states from the southern states.

Several of America's leading lawmakers at that time were originally from New Hampshire. Daniel Webster was one of them. He became a United States senator. Webster worked to prevent war between the North and the South. Senator John Parker Hale also was a New Hampshirite. Hale was one of the strongest senators against slavery.

John Parker Hale was born in Rochester, New Hampshire.

In 1853, New Hampshire sent the fourteenth president to the White House. His name was Franklin Pierce. He did not fight slavery as John Parker Hale did. Pierce did not want to anger the South. He signed a law that let the people in each western territory decide about slavery. Pierce's efforts held off war between the North and the South for a few more years.

Shortly after Abraham Lincoln became president, the Civil War (1861-1865) began. That was a war between the northern (Union) and southern

(Confederate) states. About 40,000 New Hampshirites fought for the North. Thaddeus S. C. Lowe of New Hampshire was a balloonist. He organized a balloon fleet that spied on southern troops from the sky.

Thaddeus S.C. Lowe was born near Jefferson, New Hampshire.

The North won the Civil War in 1865. Nearly 5,000 New Hampshirites had died in the northern cause. Slavery was outlawed in the United States the year the war ended.

THE GROWTH OF MANUFACTURING

Meanwhile, manufacturing (making products) became important in New Hampshire. Textiles (cloth making) became a large industry. Benjamin Prichard began a cotton mill at Manchester around 1809. It was called the Amoskeag Company. By 1850, about 15,000 people worked for Amoskeag.

By the middle 1800s, the Amoskeag Company was making other things besides cotton. One of the company's plants made steam fire engines (left).

Summer vacationers in Northwood (above) enjoyed rides on the local stagecoach. The first Concord coach was made in 1827.

New Hampshire's first shoe factory began in 1823, at Weare. Others followed. By the late 1800s, New Hampshire was a big producer of textiles, shoes, and paper and wood products. Concord made the Concord coach. Many people traveled to the West in those coaches. The coaches also carried the United States mail across the country. Portsmouth made clipper ships. These were fast, beautiful sailing ships. They took people and goods quickly across the seas.

The growth of factories brought another change to the state. Nearly all of New Hampshire's colonial families had come from England or Scotland.

During the 1800s, people from many nations came to work in New Hampshire's factories. Thousands of French Canadians arrived. Their families had moved to Canada from France. People also arrived from Ireland, Germany, Norway, Sweden, Greece, Poland, and Italy.

NEW HAMPSHIRE IN WAR, PEACE, AND POLITICS

In 1917, the United States entered World War I (1914-1918). The Portsmouth Navy Yard built submarines and warships. More than 20,000 New Hampshirites helped the United States and its allies win the war.

About seven hundred New Hampshirites died in World War I.

Since 1920, New Hampshire has held America's earliest presidential primary election. Those elections, held in many states, help decide the final candidates for president. New Hampshire's primary is held in February, before any other state's primary. New Hampshire is often called the "Primary State."

Between 1929 and 1939, America suffered through some hard times. This period is called the Great Depression. Many New Hampshire businesses had to close. By 1931, two out of every ten New Hampshire workers had lost their jobs. Natural disasters made things worse. The spring of 1936 brought floods. Hundreds of families lost their homes. In September 1938, a hurricane struck. Together, the flood and the hurricane caused over $58 million in damages.

World War II (1939-1945) helped end the Great Depression. The United States entered the war in 1941. About 60,000 New Hampshire men and women served their country. Ships and submarines made in New Hampshire also helped win the war.

Near the end of World War II, plans were laid for the United Nations (UN). Its purpose was, and still is, to work for world peace. Delegates from forty-four nations met in 1944 at Bretton Woods. That is in New Hampshire's White Mountains.

RECENT DEVELOPMENTS

Many New Hampshirites work in tourism and manufacturing. Millions of tourists visit the state each year. They enjoy the cool summers, the fall colors, and winter skiing. New hotels and motels have opened throughout the state. Ski resorts have opened in the mountains. Since 1950, several new products have been made in New Hampshire. They include televisions and computers.

New Hampshirites also helped give birth to the space age. The first American in space was Alan B. Shepard, Jr., from Derry. He made his famous journey on May 5, 1961. On January 28, 1986, the United States launched the first ordinary citizen toward space. She was Concord high-school teacher Christa McAuliffe. The world eagerly awaited her lessons from space. But her *Challenger* spacecraft exploded after launch. McAuliffe and the six astronauts aboard were killed.

Hard times again hit New Hampshire in the 1990s. Many dairy farmers went out of business. Large numbers of factory workers and loggers were laid off. The state government was in need of money. Once again, New Hampshirites must be tough as granite.

Above: Bretton Woods Conference delegates posed for this picture in July 1944.

Alan B. Shepard, Jr., (above) made the third manned landing on the moon in 1971.

New Hampshirites
and Their
Work

New Hampshirites and Their Work

The United States Census counted 1,109,252 New Hampshirites in 1990. Only ten states have fewer people. About one-third of New Hampshirites have French-Canadian ancestors. New Hampshire has one of the largest French-Canadian populations in the nation. The ancestors of many other New Hampshirites came from the British Isles. Others came from Germany, Norway, Sweden, Greece, Poland, and Italy. About 98 percent of all New Hampshirites are white. But small numbers of African Americans, American Indians, Asians, and Hispanics also live there.

New Hampshire's Government

The United States is a democracy—a place where the people rule themselves. New Hampshire is one of our most democratic states. It is famous for its town meetings. Once a year, the townspeople choose their officials at those meetings. They also decide other local matters. These include such things as the town's budget and road repairs. Town

Opposite: Girls walking a fence in Andover

Some of New Hampshire's French Canadian families speak both English and French. There are French-language newspapers and radio stations in New Hampshire.

Snow sliding is a popular pastime during New Hampshire winters (below).

A town meeting in Washington, New Hampshire

meetings have been held in New Hampshire since the 1600s.

New Hampshire's legislature is called the General Court. It has two parts. One is the twenty-four-member Senate. The other is the four-hundred-member House of Representatives. Only one United States lawmaking body has more members. That one is the United States House of Representatives. Why does such a small state have such a big House of Representatives? In that way, a large number of New Hampshirites can take part in government.

New Hampshirites at Work

Some New Hampshirites make their living by farming (left) or fishing (right).

About 120,000 New Hampshirites have jobs making products. They make many kinds of things. Major products include computers, television and radio parts, and other kinds of machinery. They also

make car and aircraft parts, paper, and shoes. Another 120,000 New Hampshirites sell products.

Yet another 120,000 New Hampshirites work in the service industry. Nurses, lawyers, bankers, and auto mechanics are all service workers. People who take care of tourists are also service workers. They include hotel, motel, resort, and restaurant workers. About 70,000 New Hampshire service workers also do government work.

About 3,000 New Hampshire families live on farms. Milk is the state's top farm product. New Hampshire is a leading producer of maple syrup. Eggs, beef cattle, apples, and potatoes are other important farm products.

Smaller numbers of New Hampshirites make a living by fishing or mining. Those who fish catch lobsters, clams, cod, and flounder. The miners mine sand, gravel, and, of course, granite.

Logging (left) employs several thousand New Hampshire people. The state is a leading producer of maple syrup (right).

About 10 million tourists visit New Hampshire each year. That is nearly ten times as many people as live there!

Overleaf: A northern New Hampshire farm

A Trip Through the Granite State

A Trip Through the Granite State

There are good reasons why so many people visit New Hampshire. The state has lovely little towns. It has historic sites at almost every turn. Something about New Hampshire's countryside stirs the soul. Many people travel a thousand miles or more for the quiet beauty of its lakes and mountains.

The Four Oldest Towns

Its short seacoast is a good place to start a trip through New Hampshire. Dover, Portsmouth, Exeter, and Hampton all lie near the ocean. They are the Granite State's four oldest towns.

Dover has the oldest family farm in America. It is called the Tuttle farm. It dates from 1632. The Tuttle family has worked the farm for 360 years! The John Parker Hale House can be visited in Dover. Hale lived there for about thirty years.

Portsmouth is south of Dover. It is New Hampshire's fifth-largest city. An outdoor museum called Strawbery Banke is in Portsmouth. The old houses there show how the town has changed since

Fishing boats in Portsmouth

the 1600s. The John Paul Jones House is also in Portsmouth. Jones was a famous sailor who helped America win the Revolutionary War. He lived in Portsmouth while the warship *Ranger* was being built.

To the southwest is Exeter. It is home to a famous "prep school." The school is called Phillips Exeter Academy. Among its students were Daniel Webster and Franklin Pierce. The Front Street Historic District in Exeter has homes dating from the 1700s.

The Tuck Memorial Museum is in nearby Hampton. Visitors can see a one-room schoolhouse

"Prep schools" provide only classes that prepare young people for college.

*Left: Phillips Exeter Academy, in Exeter
Right: The John Paul Jones House, in Portsmouth*

These fifers and drummers wore Revolutionary War uniforms when they marched in a Concord parade.

and an early fire station. The museum also has old farm equipment, toys, and other items from pioneer times.

THE THREE LARGEST CITIES

Manchester, Nashua, and Concord are New Hampshire's largest cities. All three are in the southern part of New Hampshire. They lie along the Merrimack River.

People from Massachusetts settled Derryfield in 1722. The town was later named for Manchester, England. Manchester is now the state's largest city.

About half its people are French Canadian. The weekly French-language newspaper *L'Action* is published in Manchester. Another Manchester newspaper is the *Union Leader*.

John Stark's home is in Manchester. Stark died there at the age of ninety-three. He was the last living American Revolutionary War general. New Hampshire's leading art museum is also in Manchester. It is called the Currier Gallery of Art. Old Amoskeag Company buildings can also be seen in Manchester. They date back to when the company was the world's leading textile maker.

New Hampshire's second-biggest city is Nashua. It is south of Manchester. Nashua was settled in 1673. In 1987, a national magazine chose the city as America's best place to live. The Robert Frost homestead is in Derry, outside Nashua. Frost was one of America's great poets.

Concord is north of Manchester. It was founded in 1727. Concord has been the state capital since 1808. Visitors can watch the state lawmakers at work in the capitol. Outside the building stand statues of Daniel Webster, John Parker Hale, John Stark, and Franklin Pierce. President Pierce's home can be seen in the city. Concord is New Hampshire's third-largest city.

The interior of the state capitol, in Concord

Christa McAuliffe (top) was the first private citizen to be a passenger on a space shuttle. The marker stands at Concord High School, where she taught social studies.

There is a marker under a tree at Concord High School. It says: "I touch the future—I teach. Christa McAuliffe, September 2, 1948-January 28, 1986." It reminds people that Christa McAuliffe was more than a space traveler. She was a social studies teacher at Concord High School. Her students thought very highly of her.

OTHER SOUTHERN NEW HAMPSHIRE HIGHLIGHTS

The Cathedral of the Pines is in Rindge, west of Nashua. It is an outdoor place of worship. People of all religions are welcome there. The cathedral was founded in 1945 by a couple who had lost a son in World War II. It honors the men and women who died in America's wars.

Peterborough is north of the Cathedral of the Pines. This town has a special honor. What is thought to be America's oldest public library is located there. It was founded in 1833. Today, a history magazine for children is published in Peterborough. It is called *Cobblestone*.

Franklin Pierce's and Daniel Webster's childhood homes are in southern New Hampshire. The Pierce Homestead is in Hillsboro. The Webster Birthplace is in Franklin.

Shaker Village is in Canterbury. Ann Lee founded the Shakers in England about 1772. It was a religious group. The name came from their habit of shaking while they danced during worship. The Shaker community in Canterbury began in 1792. At Shaker Village, visitors can see Shaker buildings, furniture, and crafts.

The Shakers invented clothespins.

About fifty covered bridges can be seen in New Hampshire. Most of them were built during the 1800s. Young couples of those days would stop under covered bridges and kiss. That is why the structures were called "kissing bridges." One famous covered bridge dates from 1866. The bridge links the towns of Cornish, New Hampshire, and Windsor, Vermont. This bridge is about 450 feet

Shaker Village, in Canterbury

This covered bridge in Jackson is one of the state's fifty or so covered bridges.

long. It is the longest covered bridge still in use in the United States.

CENTRAL AND NORTHERN NEW HAMPSHIRE

It is also said that Winnipesaukee means "beautiful water in a high place."

Central New Hampshire is a land of lakes and hills. The state's largest lake is in this region. The Indians named the lake *Winnipesaukee.* The name may mean "the smile of the Great Spirit." Today, the lake is a popular place to boat, fish, and swim.

The White Mountains are north of Lake Winnipesaukee. They were named for their rocky peaks. The peaks look white in the sunlight. The

Old Man of the Mountains is in the White Mountains. Surveyors first saw the Old Man's granite head in 1805. The Old Man has been New Hampshire's official emblem since 1945.

The Flume is near the Old Man. It is a narrow canyon. A path leads visitors through the Flume. Ninety-three-year-old "Aunt" Jess Guernsey discovered the Flume in 1803. She was fishing at the time. The Old Man and the Flume are in the mountain gap called Franconia Notch.

Many cities have streets named for United States presidents. New Hampshire has done that with its mountain peaks. The peaks are in the Presidential Range of the White Mountains. They

Left: Ice on the summit of Mount Washington
Right: The Flume

The Mount Washington Cog Railway takes people to the top of the mountain.

Winds from tornadoes are stronger than winds from hurricanes, but who would measure them?

include Mounts Washington, Adams, Jefferson, Madison, and Monroe. Those names honor the first five presidents of the United States.

A cog railway takes people to the top of Mount Washington. That is New England's highest peak. From the top, visitors can look *down* on the clouds. Tourists can go up Mount Washington only in warm weather. But scientists work year-round at a weather station there.

Mount Washington has some of the worst winter weather in the nation. Temperatures often dip down to minus 30 degrees Fahrenheit. Winter winds usually blow at 60 miles per hour or more. The strongest wind ever measured on earth was on Mount Washington. It hit during a storm on April 12, 1934. The wind reached 231 miles per hour! Not even hurricanes have been measured with winds that strong.

The White Mountains reach into far northern New Hampshire. New Hampshirites call this area the "North Country." The largest town is Berlin. It has only 12,000 people. The North Country has lovely woodlands and crystal-clear air.

Many interesting animals live in the North Country. Bears and moose roam the woods and mountains. Visitors might see bobcats. Beavers can

be spotted along the streams and lakes. Deer, foxes, raccoons, and porcupines are found there.

During the 1800s, the North Country was the scene of an interesting event. New Hampshire's northern tip juts into Canada. Both the United States and Canada wanted this piece of land. The two countries argued. But in 1832, the people of the region decided to form their own country. They called it the Indian Stream Republic. It didn't last long. In 1842, the Webster-Ashburton Treaty was signed. That made the region part of the United States. A marker in the town of Pittsburg tells the Indian Stream Republic's strange story.

Moose (above) and beavers (below) are among the many animals that live in New Hampshire.

A Gallery of Famous
New Hampshirites

A GALLERY OF FAMOUS NEW HAMPSHIRITES

New Hampshire has produced many famous people. There are two reasons for that. First, New Hampshire is one of our oldest states. Second, New Hampshire had some of early America's best schools.

Passaconaway (1565?-1665?) was a Pennacook Indian chief. His people claimed that he could turn himself into fire. They said that he could turn the trees green in winter. But when the English arrived, that changed. Passaconaway said that the English were stronger than his magic. He became a peace-keeper between the Indians and the settlers. Passaconaway was about one hundred when he died. It was said that wolves pulled a sled containing his body to the top of Mount Washington. Then, the sled and the wolves disappeared in a cloud of fire.

John Stark (1728-1822) was born in Londonderry, New Hampshire. He was captured by Indians as a young man. The Indians liked the way their young prisoner fought them. He didn't beg for mercy. The Indians adopted him for a time. Stark later served with Rogers' Rangers during the

Passaconaway

Opposite: A statue of President Franklin Pierce in front of the state capitol

47

French and Indian War. He is most famous as New Hampshire's greatest hero of the Revolutionary War. General Stark also made up New Hampshire's famous motto: "Live Free or Die."

The great statesman **Daniel Webster** (1782-1852) was born in Salisbury, now called Franklin. In 1801, Webster graduated from Dartmouth College. He was known for his stirring speeches. As a U.S. senator, he once said, "Liberty and Union, now and forever, one and inseparable!" Webster was saying that the nation had to prevent a civil war. Later, as U.S. secretary of state, he helped make the Webster-Ashburton Treaty. That settled a border dispute between the United States and Canada.

Statesman Daniel Webster (left) and newspaper editor Horace Greeley (right) were New Hampshire natives.

Sarah Josepha Hale (1788-1879) was born in Newport. When she was thirty-four, her husband died. Mrs. Hale had five children and not enough money. She became a writer and a magazine editor. She wrote the poem "Mary Had a Little Lamb." Sarah Josepha Hale also worked to have Thanksgiving made into a national holiday. That finally happened in 1863.

Franklin Pierce (1804-1869) was born in Hillsboro. He was a political "boy wonder." When Pierce was only twenty-five, he was elected to the New Hampshire House of Representatives. At thirty-three, he became the youngest member of the U.S. Senate. Pierce later became one of the youngest presidents of the United States. He was forty-eight when he took office. Only Theodore Roosevelt, John F. Kennedy, and Bill Clinton were younger.

Horace Greeley (1811-1872) was born in Amherst. He became a leader in the movement to end slavery. Greeley used the *New York Tribune* to fight slavery. He founded that newspaper in 1841. He also felt that the western part of the nation had a big future. He came up with the phrase "Go West, young man." In 1870, Horace Greeley helped found Greeley, Colorado. The town was named for him.

Author and editor
Sarah Josepha Hale

Laura Bridgman (right) became the first blind and deaf person in the country to be educated.

Mary Baker Eddy (1821-1910) was born on a farm in Bow, near Concord. Her health was poor. She believed that prayer and Bible study made her feel better. In 1879, Mrs. Eddy founded a new religion called Christian Science. It teaches that prayer and an understanding of God can cure illness. There are now three thousand Christian Science churches worldwide.

Laura Bridgman (1829-1889) was born in Hanover. An illness left her deaf and blind at the age of two. At that time, most people felt that children who were deaf and blind couldn't learn. Laura proved them wrong. She learned to read by feeling raised letters. She "heard" by having words spelled on her hand. She learned to "speak" by spelling words with her fingers. Laura Bridgman was America's first highly educated blind and deaf child.

Daniel Chester French (1850-1931) was born in Exeter. He became a sculptor. Between 1873 and 1875, French made *The Minute Man*. That famous statue of a Revolutionary War soldier stands in Concord, Massachusetts. He also made the great Abraham Lincoln statue at the Lincoln Memorial in Washington, D.C. French worked on that statue for eleven years, from 1911 to 1922.

Left: Religious leader Mary Baker Eddy
Right: Sculptor Daniel Chester French

Two chief justices of the U.S. Supreme Court were born in New Hampshire. **Salmon Portland Chase** (1808-1873) was born in Cornish. **Harlan Fiske Stone** (1872-1946) was born in Chesterfield. Another New Hampshirite, **David Souter,** became a Supreme Court justice in 1990. He was born in Massachusetts in 1939. But Souter's family moved to a New Hampshire farm when he was eleven.

Skier **Barbara Ann Cochran** was born in Claremont in 1951. She won a gold medal at the 1972 Winter Olympics. Baseball star **Carlton Fisk** was born in Vermont in 1947. But he grew up in Charlestown, New Hampshire. In 1990, Fisk set the

Above: United States Supreme Court justice David Souter
Below: Olympic gold medal skier Barbara Ann Cochran

all-time record for homers by a catcher. He did it by belting his 328th home run. He was playing for the Chicago White Sox at the time.

Home to Chief Passaconaway and General John Stark, Laura Bridgman and Carlton Fisk, and astronauts Alan B. Shepard, Jr., and Christa McAuliffe . . .

The state that formed the first government free of England, that voted the U.S. Constitution into effect, and that was struck by the strongest wind ever measured on earth . . .

A land of stone walls, covered bridges, lovely lakes and woods, and the Old Man of the Mountains . . .

This is New Hampshire—the Granite State!

Did You Know?

"New Hampshire Reds" are not a sports team, but a breed of chickens developed in New Hampshire in the early 1900s.

Betty and Barney Hill, a New Hampshire couple, claimed they were taken aboard a flying saucer not far from the Old Man of the Mountains.

Four signers of the Declaration of Independence were doctors. Two of them were New Hampshirites—Dr. Josiah Bartlett and Dr. Matthew Thornton.

Captain Joseph McConnell, Jr., who was born in Dover, was the top combat pilot of the Korean War. He shot down sixteen enemy planes.

Carlton Fisk was called "The Catcher who Changed His Sox" after going from the Boston Red Sox to the Chicago White Sox in 1981.

Laban Ainsworth served as a minister at Jaffrey, New Hampshire, for seventy-six and a half years. Reverend Ainsworth died in 1858 at the age of one hundred.

Circus owner P. T. Barnum called the view from the top of Mount Washington "the second greatest show on earth." He called his circus "The Greatest Show on Earth."

A pet cat named Inga was once picked up by a wind atop Mount Washington and set down 20 feet away in a snowbank.

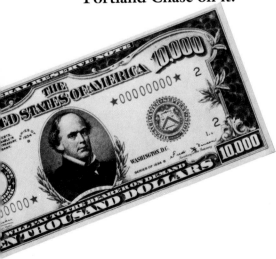

The $10,000 bill that was once printed by the United States Treasury had a picture of Salmon Portland Chase on it.

The first college boat race was held between teams from Harvard and Yale in 1853 on Lake Winnipesaukee.

A young Manchester man, George Washington Morrison Nutt, went on tour in the 1800s as "The Smallest Man in the World." Nutt was only 2 feet 5 inches tall.

New Hampshire has towns named Rye and Sandwich.

Joseph Glidden, who was born in Charlestown, invented barbed wire in 1873, in Illinois.

New Hampshire's 18-mile coastline is the shortest coast of any state that lies along an ocean.

NEW HAMPSHIRE INFORMATION

State Flag

Purple finch

Purple lilacs

Area: 9,297 square miles (only six states are smaller; forty-three are larger)

Greatest Distance North to South: 180 miles

Greatest Distance East to West: 93 miles

Coastline: 18 miles

Borders: Canada's province of Quebec to the north; Maine and the Atlantic Ocean to the east; Massachusetts to the south; Vermont and a small part of Quebec to the west

Highest Point: Mount Washington, 6,288 feet above sea level (the highest point in New England)

Lowest Point: Sea level, along the Atlantic Ocean

Hottest Recorded Temperature: 106° F. (at Nashua, on the Fourth of July, 1911)

Coldest Recorded Temperature: -46° F. (at Pittsburg, on January 28, 1925)

Statehood: The ninth state, on June 21, 1788

Origin of Name: New Hampshire was named for the county of Hampshire in England

Capital: Concord

Counties: 10

United States Senators: 2

United States Representatives: 2 (as of 1992)

State Senators: 24

State Representatives: 400 (the largest house of representatives of any state)

State Song: "Old New Hampshire," by John F. Holmes (words) and Maurice Hoffman (music)

State Motto: "Live Free or Die"

Main Nickname: "Granite State"

Other Nicknames: "White Mountain State," "Switzerland of America," "Primary State"

State Emblem: The Old Man of the Mountains (since 1945)

State Flag: Adopted in 1909   **State Tree:** White birch

State Seal: Adopted in 1931   **State Animal:** White-tailed deer

State Flower: Purple lilac   **State Insect:** Ladybug

State Bird: Purple finch   **State Rock:** Granite

Mountains: White Mountains

Some Rivers: Connecticut, Merrimack, Piscataqua, Androscoggin, Pemigewasset, Saco

Lakes: Winnipesaukee, Connecticut, Squam, Ossipee

Islands: The three southernmost of the Isles of Shoals

National Forest: White Mountain National Forest

Wildlife: Deer, bears, moose, foxes, beavers, raccoons, rabbits, porcupines, chipmunks, otters, skunks, bobcats, purple finches, ducks, geese, pheasants, grouse, sea gulls, many other kinds of birds, snapping turtles and other turtles, rattlesnakes and other snakes, many kinds of frogs and toads, trout, bass, perch, and many other kinds of fish

Fishing Products: Lobsters, clams, cod, flounder

Farm Products: Milk, eggs, beef cattle, apples, potatoes, maple syrup, blueberries, hay, sweet corn, Christmas trees

Mining Products: Sand, gravel, granite

Manufacturing Products: Computers and many other kinds of machinery, car and aircraft parts, television and radio parts, paper and wood products, shoes and other leather goods, food products

Population: 1,109,252, fortieth among the fifty states (1990 U.S. Census Bureau figures)

Major Cities (1990 Census):

Manchester	99,567	Rochester	26,630
Nashua	79,662	Portsmouth	25,925
Concord	36,006	Salem	25,746
Derry	29,603	Dover	25,042

The Old Man of the Mountains

Ladybug

White birch trees

New Hampshire History

8000 B.C.—Prehistoric Indians live in New Hampshire

1603—Martin Pring of England is the first known explorer in New Hampshire

1605—French explorer Samuel de Champlain sails along the New Hampshire coast

1614—English captain John Smith explores New Hampshire's coastline and the Isles of Shoals

1622—Englishman John Mason receives a large amount of land that becomes New Hampshire

1623—David Thomson builds a settlement at present-day Rye; Edward and William Hilton start Dover

1631—Strawbery Banke (present-day Portsmouth) is founded

1638—Exeter and Hampton are founded

1641—New Hampshire becomes part of Massachusetts

1673—Nashua (then called Dunstable) is settled

1679—New Hampshire becomes a royal colony

1700—New Hampshire has about 5,000 settlers

1722—Manchester (then called Derryfield) is settled

1727—Concord (then called Pennycook) is founded

1741—Benning Wentworth is named royal governor

1756—New Hampshire's first newspaper, the *New Hampshire Gazette*, is founded at Portsmouth

1761—New Hampshire's first stagecoach begins running

1763—England wins the French and Indian War

1769—Dartmouth College is founded

1775—The Revolutionary War begins

1776—New Hampshire forms the first state government that is totally free of England

1783—The United States wins the Revolutionary War

1788—New Hampshire becomes the ninth state

1800—New Hampshire's population reaches about 184,000

1808—Concord becomes New Hampshire's permanent capital

1833—What is thought to be America's oldest public library is founded at Peterborough

1853—New Hampshire's Franklin Pierce becomes the fourteenth president of the United States

1861-65—About 40,000 New Hampshirites help the North win the Civil War

1866—The University of New Hampshire is founded

1900—The Granite State's population is about 412,000

1917-18—After the United States enters World War I, more than 20,000 New Hampshirites serve

1934—The strongest wind ever measured on earth hits Mount Washington, reaching 231 miles per hour

1936—Floods destroy more than $8 million in property

1938—The New England Hurricane does over $50 million worth of damage to New Hampshire

1941-45—After the United States enters World War II, 60,000 New Hampshire men and women serve

1959—The Kancamagus Highway through the White Mountains opens

1961—Alan B. Shepard, Jr., becomes the first American in space

1964—New Hampshire begins a lottery to help pay for education

1986—New Hampshire high-school teacher Christa McAuliffe is killed when the space shuttle *Challenger* explodes

1988—Happy two hundredth birthday, Granite State!

1990—The state's first nuclear power plant begins operating at Seabrook

1993—New Hampshire celebrates Martin Luther King, Jr. Day for the first time

1995—Residents of Langdon build a new school on a volunteer basis because there were no government funds available

America's oldest public library, in Peterborough

MAP KEY

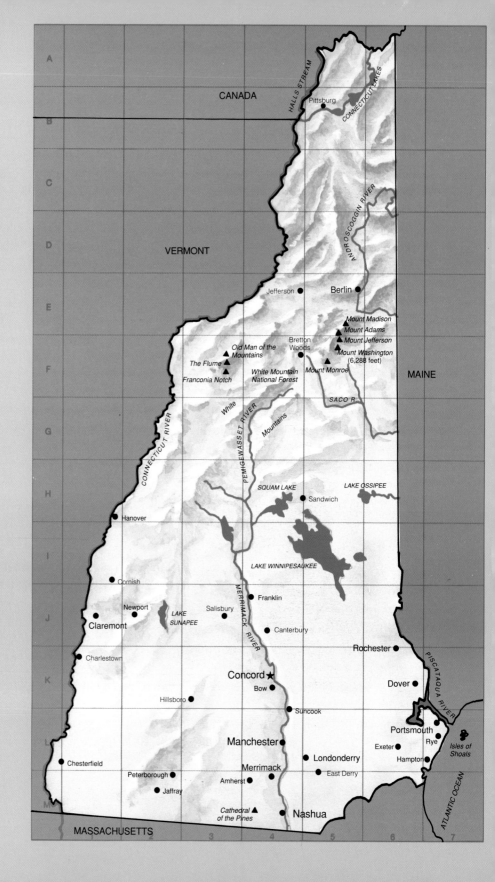

GLOSSARY

allies: Nations that help one another

ancestor: A person from whom one is descended, such as a grandfather or a great-grandmother

ancient: Relating to a time early in history

antislavery: Against slavery

astronaut: A person who is highly trained for spaceflight

candidate: A person who runs for office

canyon: A deep, steep-sided valley

capital: The city that is the seat of government

capitol: The building in which the government meets

climate: The typical weather of a region

coast: The land along a large body of water

colonist: A person who leaves his or her country to live in a colony

colony: A settlement that is outside a parent country and that is ruled by the parent country

constitution: A framework of government; the basic law of a country

debt: Money that is borrowed from another person or country and must be paid back

delegates: People who act for or represent others

democracy: A form of government in which the people rule themselves

explorer: A person who visits and studies unknown lands

glacier: A large mass of ice that moves slowly down a slope or over a large area of land

hurricane: A huge storm that forms over an ocean

independence: Freedom from being controlled by others

legislature: A body of lawmakers

manufacturing: The making of products

million: A thousand thousand (1,000,000)

moccasin: Soft shoes made of animal skins

patriot: A person who loves and supports his or her country

61

population: The number of people in a place

primary election: An election that helps narrow down the field of candidates for a later election

sculptor: An artist who carves, chisels, or molds hard materials

service worker: A person, such as a nurse or an auto mechanic, who serves others

settlers: People who move to an uninhabited area

slavery: A practice in which some people are owned by other people

submarines: Ships that can go underwater

surveyor: A person who measures land to determine boundaries

tourism: The business of providing services, such as food and lodging, for travelers

town meeting: A meeting in which the people of a town choose their officials and decide other local matters

PICTURE ACKNOWLEDGMENTS

Front cover, © **David Brownell;** 1, © William Johnson/**Johnson's Photography;** 2, **Tom Dunnington;** 3, © **David Brownell;** 5, **Tom Dunnington;** 6-7, © **David Brownell;** 8, © **Craig Blouin;** 9 (left), © **Bob Grant;** 9 (right), **courtesy of Hammond Incorporated, Maplewood, New Jersey;** 10, © **David Brownell;** 11 (left), © Frederick Stork/**Photri;** 11 (right), © **Bob Grant;** 12 (top), © **David Brownell;** 12 (bottom), © William Johnson/**Johnson's Photography;** 13 (left), © Clyde H. Smith/**Tony Stone Worldwide/Chicago Ltd.;** 13 (right), © **David Brownell;** 14, **New Hampshire Historical Society;** 16, © **Joseph A. DiChello, Jr.;** 17, **Historical Pictures/Stock Montage;** 18, © **David Forbert;** 19, © **Lee Foster;** 20, **North Wind Picture Archives, hand colored;** 22, © **Mae Scanlan;** 23, **New Hampshire Historical Society;** 25, **New Hampshire Historical Society;** 26, **New Hampshire Historical Society;** 29 (both pictures), **AP/Wide World Photos;** 30, © **David Brownell;** 31, © **Craig Blouin;** 32 (top), © **Craig Blouin;** 32 (bottom left), © **Craig Blouin;** 32 (bottom right), © William Johnson/**Johnson's Photography;** 33 (left), © William Johnson/**Johnson's Photography;** 33 (right), © **Bob Grant;** 34-35, © William Johnson/**Johnson's Photography;** 36, © **David Forbert;** 37 (left), © **David Forbert;** 37 (right), © William Johnson/**Johnson's Photography;** 38, © William Johnson/**Johnson's Photography;** 39, © Mark E. Gibson/**Marilyn Gartman Agency;** 40 (top), **AP/Wide World Photos;** 40 (bottom), © **David Forbert;** 41, © William Johnson/**Johnson's Photography;** 42, © Tom Mackie/**Tony Stone Worldwide/Chicago Ltd.;** 43 (left), © **Tom Till Photographer;** 43 (right), © Frederick Stork/**Photri;** 44, © John W. Warden/**SuperStock;** 45 (top), © Barbara Gerlach/**Dembinsky Photo Assoc.;** 45 (bottom), © **SuperStock;** 46, © **North Wind Pictures;** 47, **New Hampshire Historical Society;** 48 (both pictures), **AP/Wide World Photos;** 49, **North Wind Picture Archives;** 50, **Historical Pictures/Stock Montage;** 51 (left), **AP/Wide World Photos;** 51 (right), **North Wind Picture Archives;** 52 (both pictures), **AP/Wide World Photos;** 53, **AP/Wide World Photos;** 54, **University of Illinois;** 54-55, **Krause Publications, Inc., 700 E. State St., Iola, Wisconsin 54990;** 55, **courtesy of the Harvard University Archives;** 56 (top), **courtesy Flag Research Center, Winchester, Massachusetts, 01890;** 56 (middle), © William Johnson/**Johnson's Photography;** 56 (bottom), © **Craig Blouin;** 57 (top), © **Bob Grant;** 57 (middle), © **Craig Blouin;** 57 (bottom), © **SuperStock;** 59, © **David Forbert;** 60, **Tom Dunnington;** back cover, © **David Brownell**

INDEX

Page numbers in boldface type indicate illustrations.

ABOUT THE AUTHOR

Dennis Brindell Fradin is the author of 150 published children's books. His works for Childrens Press include the Young People's Stories of Our States series, the Disaster! series, and the Thirteen Colonies series. Dennis is married to Judith Bloom Fradin, who taught high-school and college English for many years. She is now Dennis's chief researcher. The Fradins are the parents of two sons, Anthony and Michael, and a daughter, Diana. Dennis graduated from Northwestern University in 1967 with a B.A. in creative writing, and has lived in Evanston, Illinois, since that year.